J362·11

D0266279

MSC
4/99

People who help us
In Hospital

Dr Janet Harbour

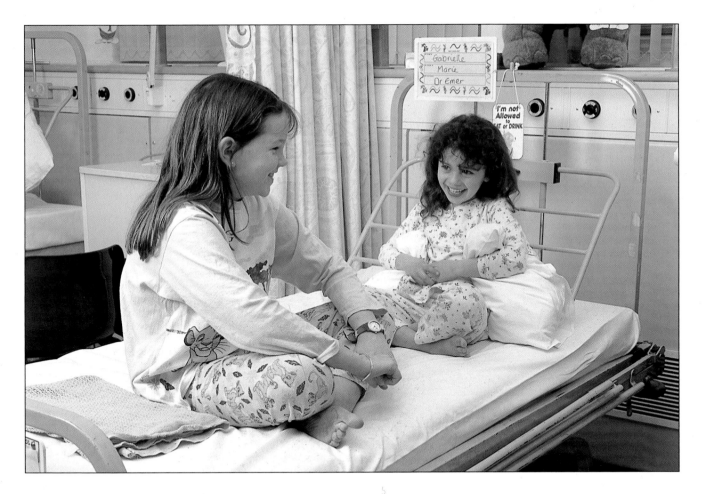

WAYLAND

Contents

**All Wayland books encourage children to read
and help them improve their literacy.**

 The contents page, page numbers, headings and index
help to locate a particular piece of information.

 The glossary reinforces alphabetic knowledge and
extends vocabulary.

✓ The books to read section suggests other books
dealing with the same subject.

Going to Hospital

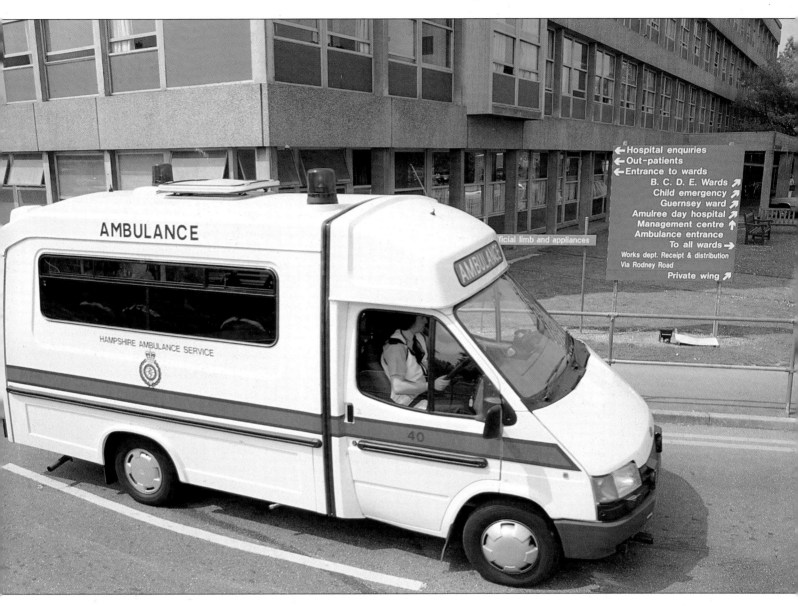

Ambulances are often used to take sick people to hospital.

An ambulance has a siren and blue warning lights and can move fast in an emergency. In hospital people are cared for by the hospital staff.

The Medical Team

The doctors are talking about how to make baby James better.

They meet each day to see every patient and to share ideas. A special machine called a **respirator** helps James to breathe through a tube.

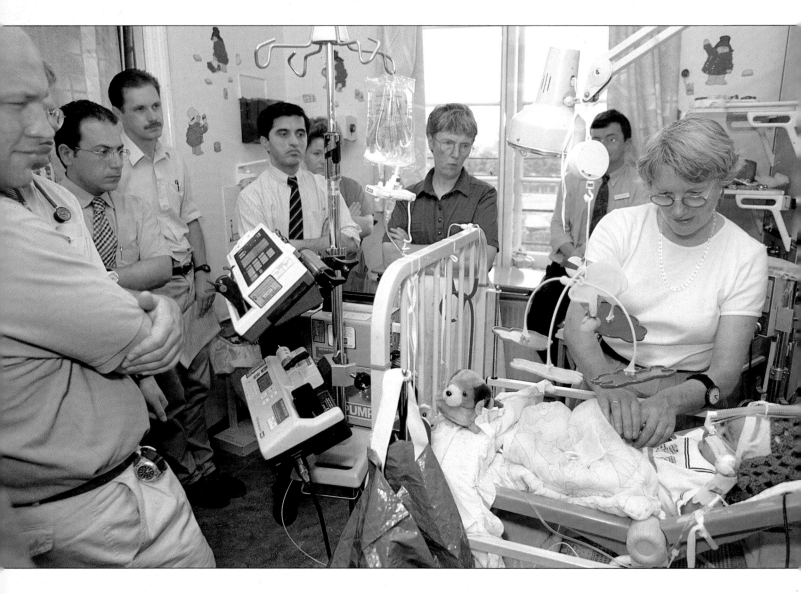

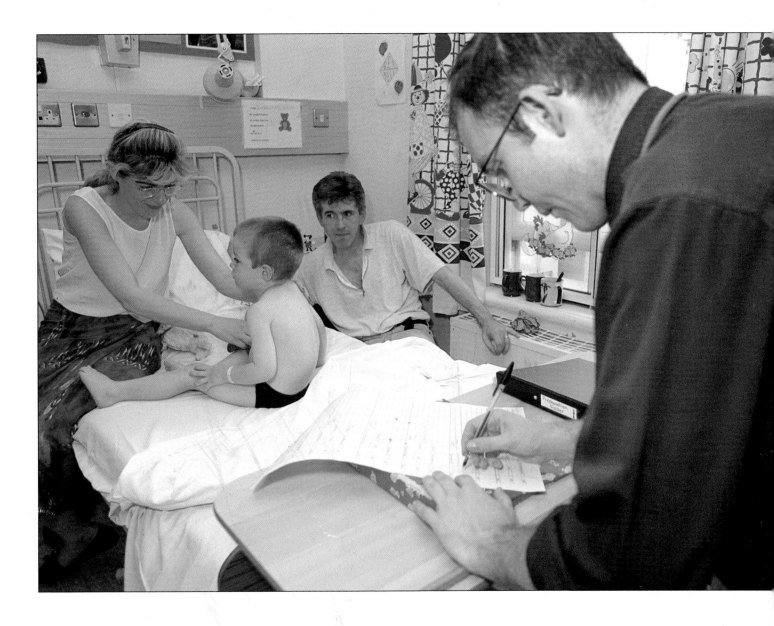

The doctor is writing down what treatment Robert should be given.

He has looked at Robert and asked questions to help find out what is wrong. The doctor can also ask for special tests to be done.

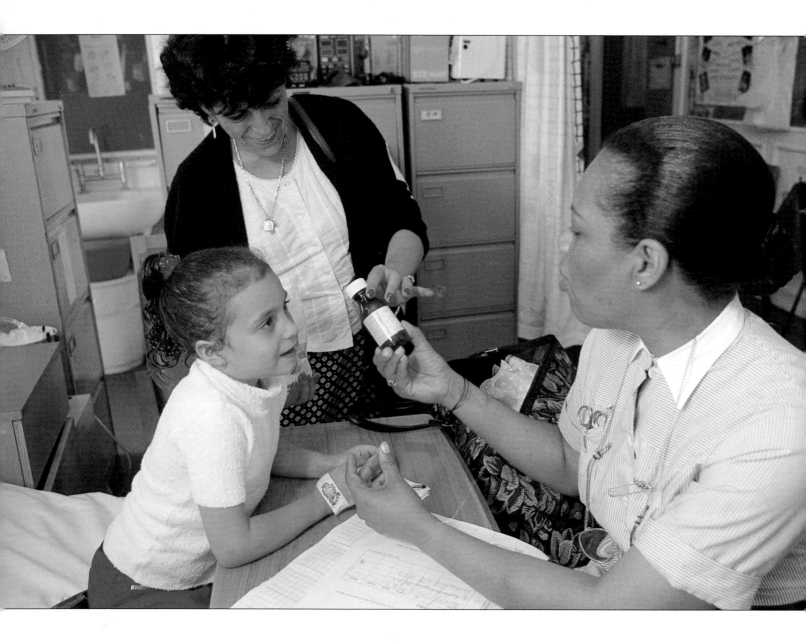

The nurse is giving out medicine.

She gives Ruby **medicine** from the bottle and explains to Ruby how it will help to make her well.

The nurse is listening to baby Claire's heart and lungs.

She is using a long tube called a **stethoscope** to help her to hear more clearly. She counts the number of heartbeats in a minute. This is called the pulse.

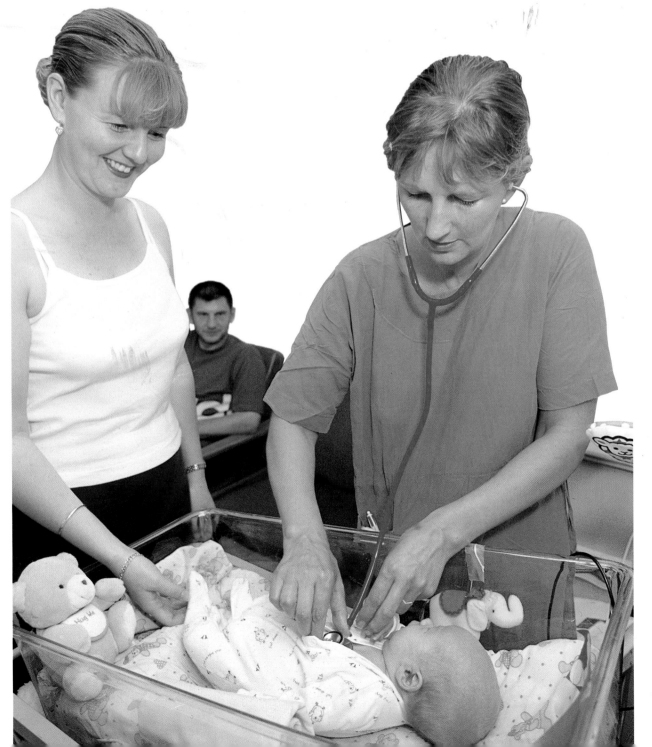

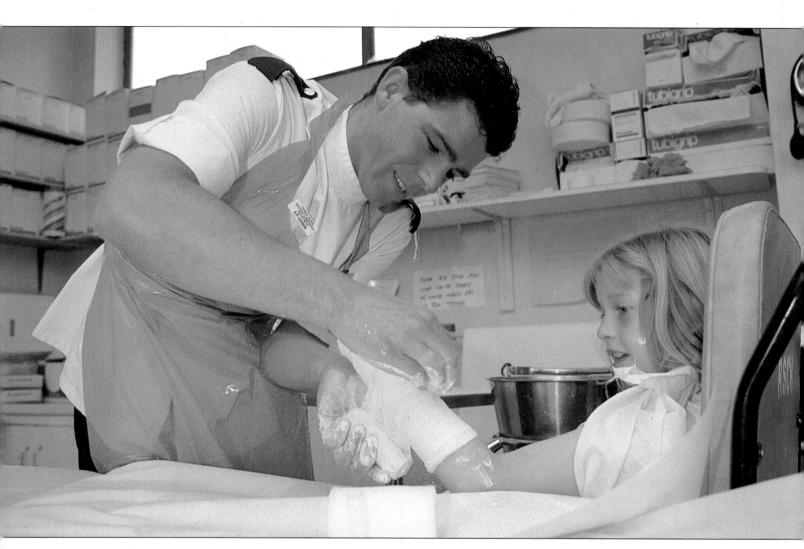

This nurse is putting a plaster bandage on Susan's broken arm.

The plaster will set hard and keep the arm straight whilst the bone is mending.

Doctors and nurses rush to help a man who is very ill.

The doctors give him **oxygen** to breathe through a mask. A nurse has put a black band on his arm to measure his **blood pressure**.

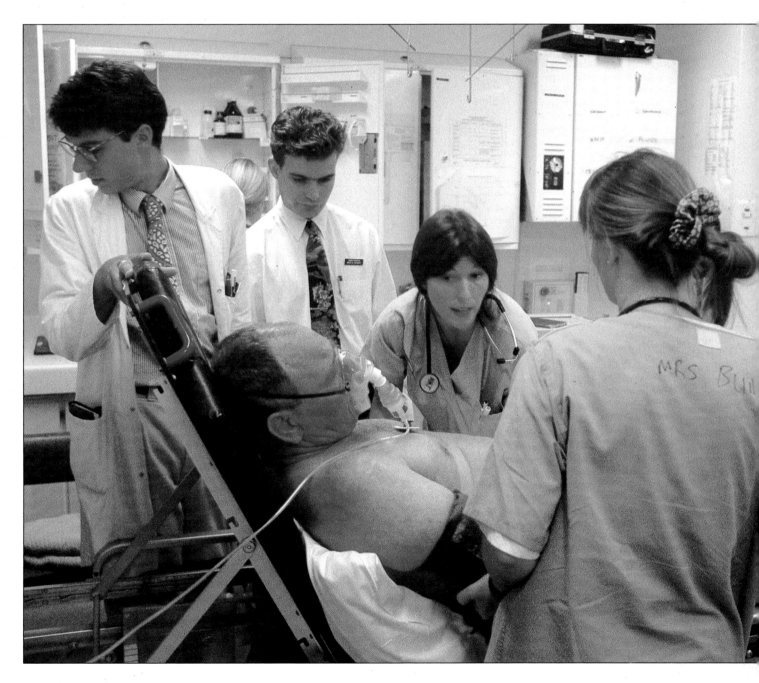

Operating Theatre Staff

The anaesthetist is putting Gunraj to sleep for an operation.

She has given a small **injection** into the back of the Gunraj's hand and is giving him special air to breathe.

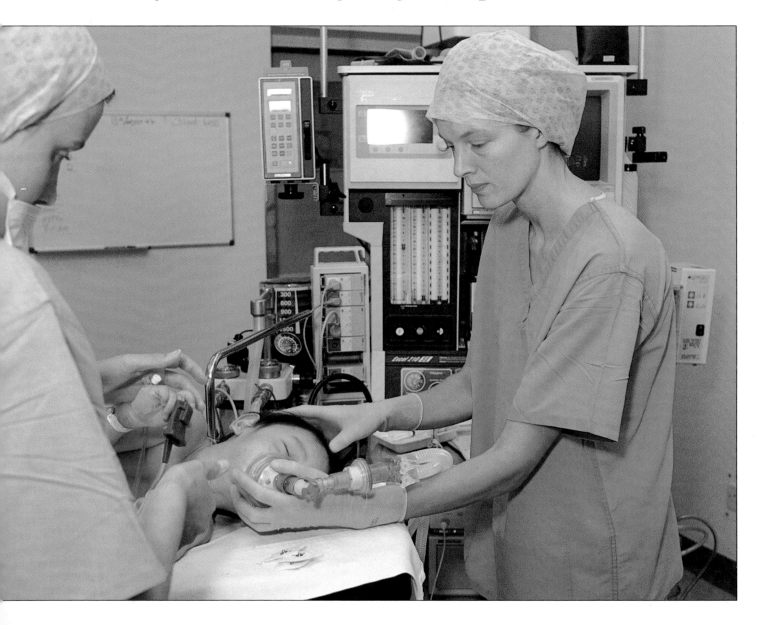

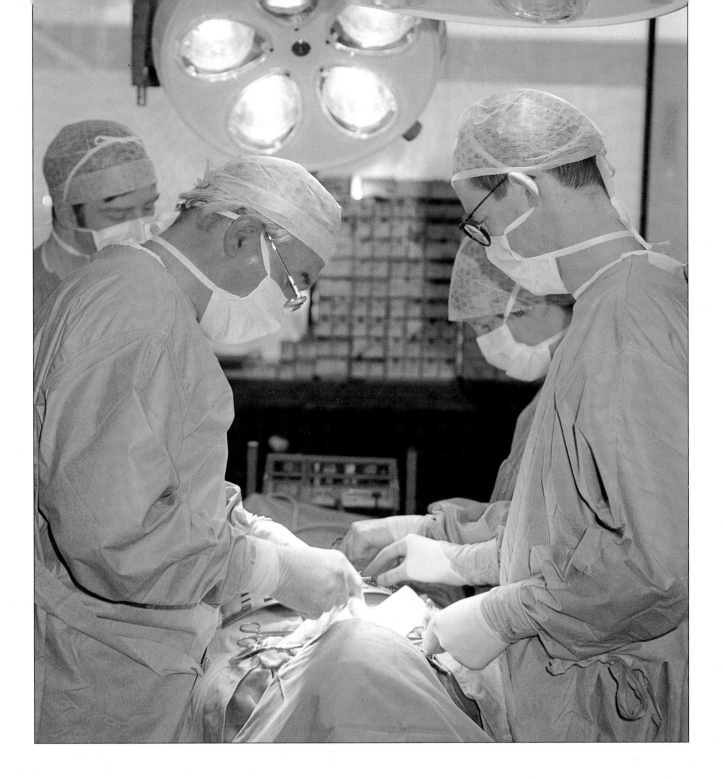

The surgeons are doing an operation.

They are repairing a part of the body which is damaged. They are wearing **sterile** masks, gloves and **gowns** to stop **germs** causing **infections**.

Pharmacy Staff

The pharmacist has put medicine into a bottle.

Another pharmacist is checking to make sure that this is the right medicine. A **prescription** written by a doctor tells the pharmacist what medicine is needed.

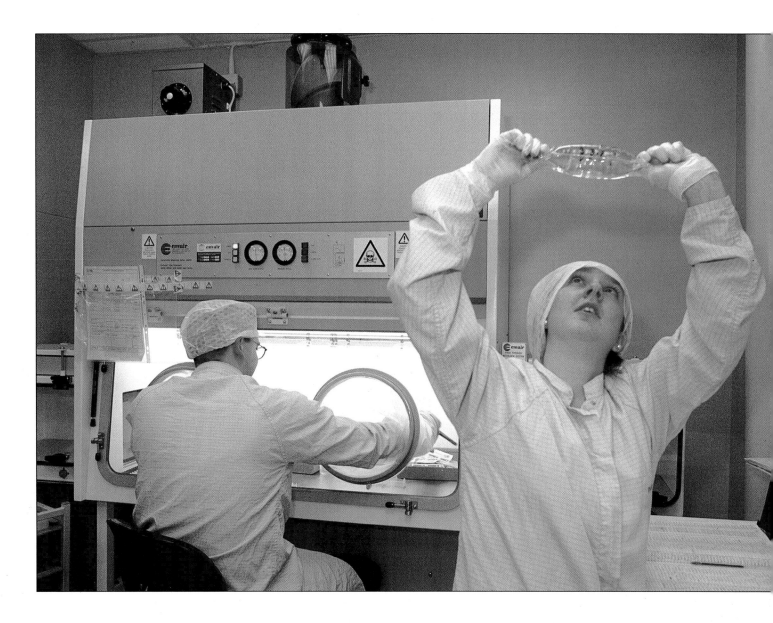

This pharmacist looks at a bag of fluid to make sure it is clear and does not leak.

This fluid will be given to a patient through a tube in their arm called a drip.

Laboratory Staff

The pathologist is looking at cells from a patient's blood.

She is using a **microscope** to make the **cells** look bigger and can tell if the cells are normal.

A pathologist can also test a patient's blood or urine.

In the laboratory special chemicals are used to do tests on samples of blood and urine from a patient. These tests help to find out what is wrong.

Physiotherapists

This physiotherapist is showing Jan how to exercise.

Exercise will make Jan's muscles strong and her joints flexible again after her illness.

The physiotherapist is clearing Paula's lungs.

She has put Paula upside down and is patting her chest to help her to cough up **mucus**.

Play Specialists

A play specialist is helping Jessica and Dan with a jigsaw puzzle.

A play specialist helps to make learning fun. Sick children play and learn together while they are in hospital.

The play specialist is helping Viren to use the computer.

Some children are missing school while they are in hospital. A computer can help Viren catch up with his lessons.

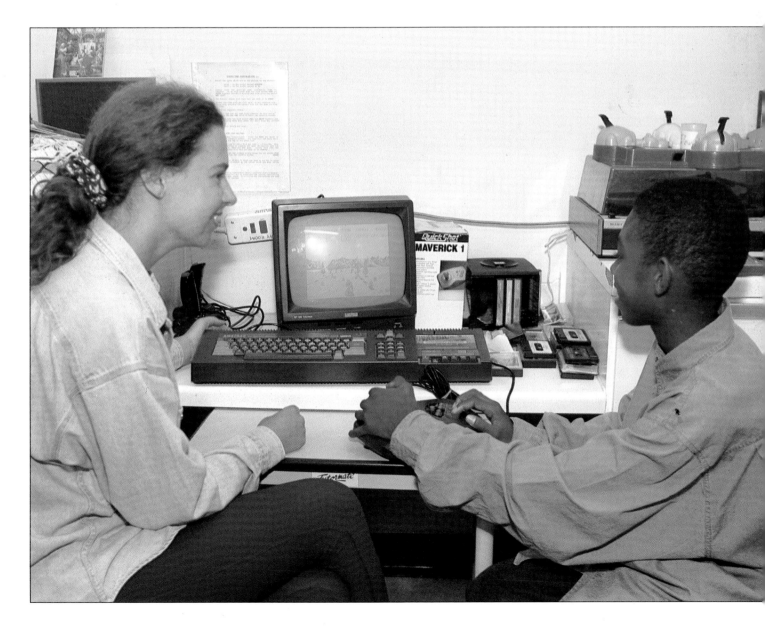

Radiographers

A radiographer is taking pictures of the inside of Mr. Davison's body.

Mr. Davison is lying down in a **scanner**. The radiographer is looking at the pictures on a computer screen.

The radiographer shows the pictures to a doctor.

Together they decide what is wrong and will write this
down in a report.

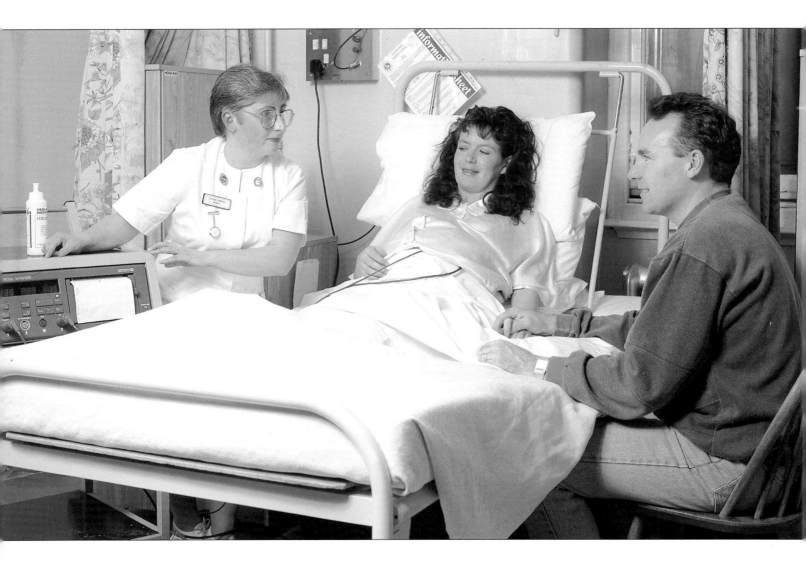

The midwife is giving advice to a couple soon to have a baby.

The midwife is checking the baby's heartbeat before the baby is born. The midwife will stay with the mother while she gives birth.

The midwife is weighing a new born baby.

The midwife checks that the baby is healthy and has put labels on the baby's ankles which shows its mother's name.

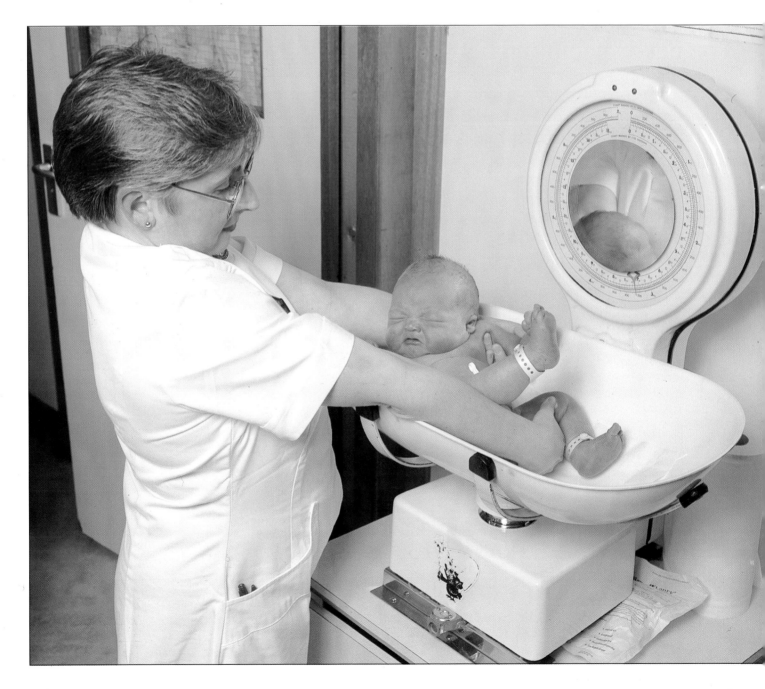

Support Staff

The dietician and chef are deciding what food to cook for the patients.

The dietician is telling the chef about patients who need special meals such as low fat or sugar-free diets.

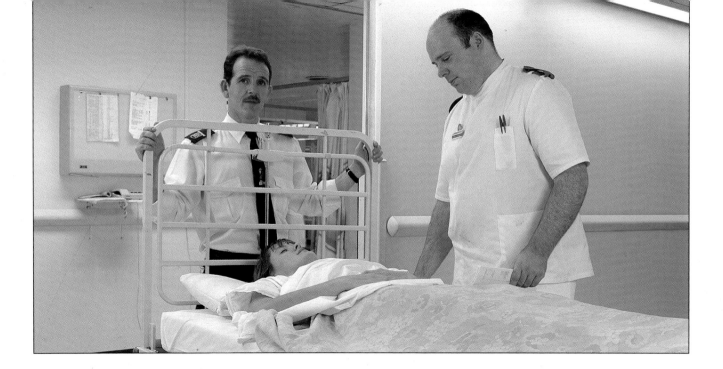

The porter is moving a patient in a hospital bed.

The porters also deliver letters and laboratory reports to the doctors and nurses around the hospital.

The laundry staff makes sure that all the dirty washing is cleaned.

All the bedsheets and white coats have to be washed and ironed. The theatre gowns have to be especially clean for operations.

The managers work in the hospital offices.

They have meetings to decide how money should be spent in the hospital.

A secretary gives the receptionist a patient's notes.

The receptionist plans when a patient can come into hospital for a check-up. The secretary writes to a patient's own doctor to say what has happened in hospital.

A clerk is putting away a patient's notes.

The notes are kept safely for when the patient comes to the hospital again.

Topic Web

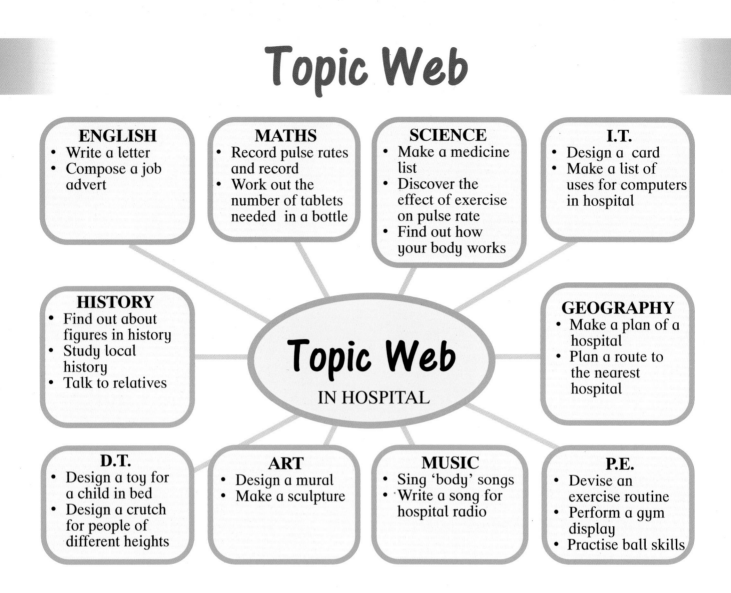

ENGLISH
- Write a letter
- Compose a job advert

MATHS
- Record pulse rates and record
- Work out the number of tablets needed in a bottle

SCIENCE
- Make a medicine list
- Discover the effect of exercise on pulse rate
- Find out how your body works

I.T.
- Design a card
- Make a list of uses for computers in hospital

HISTORY
- Find out about figures in history
- Study local history
- Talk to relatives

Topic Web

IN HOSPITAL

GEOGRAPHY
- Make a plan of a hospital
- Plan a route to the nearest hospital

D.T.
- Design a toy for a child in bed
- Design a crutch for people of different heights

ART
- Design a mural
- Make a sculpture

MUSIC
- Sing 'body' songs
- Write a song for hospital radio

P.E.
- Devise an exercise routine
- Perform a gym display
- Practise ball skills

Notes for Teachers
A hospital provides an excellent setting for many discussions and activities. Good communications are vital if mistakes are to be avoided in the hospital. This can be used to emphasis the importance of such skills and reinforced by communication exercises in a 'real context' with imaginary scenarios in the hospital. Such imaginary situations may require verbal, written or listening skills. Mathematical skills can be developed by creating problems which require a mathematical solution such as the number of nurses needed for different numbers of patients or the number of tablets needed for a given prescription.
Interpersonal skills can be developed through the discussions and activities which could include role play and group work.

Topics for discussion
The information presented can be used as the basis of discussions which cover the role of individuals, their individual responsibilities and their work as part of a team. Visitors, parents and other patients can all influence a person's stay in hospital. Ideas such as being a good patient, helping others, sharing worries and feelings, the importance of having confidence to ask questions and reporting symptoms correctly can all be included in such discussions.

There is scope to use diagrams of the body and the X-ray sections as a spring board for discussions about how individual systems in our body work and what we can do to keep ourselves healthy such as not smoking, good diet and exercise.

The section on the pharmacy can be used as a start for discussions about drugs used as medicines and harmful drugs to be avoided.

The role of midwives provides the opportunity to discuss the birth of a baby and what care it will need.

Healthy eating can be encouraged by thinking of what foods should be provided by hospital chefs.

Topic Web Activities

ENGLISH
•Speaking and listening • Writing
Pretend you are a hospital secretary and write a letter to a patient's doctor at home (their GP) about what has happened to the patient in hospital.
Working as a team of hospital managers write a job advert for a nurse saying what sort of person they should be and the sorts of skills they should have.

MATHS
• Number: Collecting, representing and interpreting data
Record pulse rates from several people and display in a graph. Compare this with results obtained after exercising. Discuss the results in terms of mean, mode and range for key stage two.
Work out the number of tablets needed in a bottle for different prescriptions.

SCIENCE
• Humans as organisms
• Experimental and investigative science
Pretend that you are a pharmacist and make a list of all the medicines you know and what they are used for.
Plan, design and carry out an experiment to show the effect of exercise on pulse rate. (Link with maths activity). Display you results on an illustrated mini-poster.
Find out about your body and how it works.

I.T.
• Communicating and handling information
Design a 'thank-you' card using a computer which could be sent to someone who works in a hospital or a 'get well' card for someone you know is ill.
Make a list of the ways that computers could be of use in hospital.

HISTORY
• Historical knowledge and understanding
• Historical enquiry • Victorian Britain
Find out about important figures in the history of hospitals eg. Florence Nightingale.
Find out about the history of your local hospital.
Talk to relatives about how medicine has changed during their lifetime.

GEOGRAPHY
• Geographical skills
Make a plan of an imaginary hospital. Describe how you would get from one part of the hospital to another.
Using a map of your nearest town work out the quickest route an ambulance can take from your home to the nearest hospital.

D.T.
• Designing and making skills
• Knowledge and understanding
Design a toy which a play specialist in a hospital could use with a child who is ill in bed.
Design a crutch which can be used for people of different heights.

ART
• Investigating and making
Design a mural for the wall of a children's ward in a hospital.
Make a sculpture for the entrance hall of the hospital.

MUSIC
• Performing and composing
Make a list of all the songs you can think of that mention body parts and sing them.
Write a song for a hospital radio station to cheer people up. Perform the song individually or in a small groups.

P.E.
• Gymnastic activities • Games
Make up a ten-minute exercise programme which patients could do in hospital and try it out with friends.
Perform a gym display which shows the movements of as many joints and muscles as possible.
Pretend you have a broken arm and practise throwing, rolling, catching and bounding the ball with a partner. Change arms and see what difference it makes.

Glossary

blood pressure   How hard the blood is pressing on the tubes (arteries) which carry it around the body.

cells   The tiny building blocks which make up living things.

germs   The very small living things which get into the body and cause illness.

gowns   Large aprons with sleeves.

infections   Illnesses which are caused by germs.

injection   When something is put into the body using a needle.

medicine   A drug that is used to treat illness.

microscope   An instrument which uses light and mirrors to make tiny things look bigger.

mucus   A sticky substance which is found in our noses and lungs. It helps to clear away any germs.

oxygen   The gas in the air which we need to breath to stay alive.

prescription   A note which the doctor writes telling the pharmacist which medicine to give to the patient.

respirator   A machine which pushes air in and out of the lungs. It is used when someone cannot breathe for themselves.

scanner   A machine for examining parts of the body.

sterile   Clean and free from germs.

stethoscope   A hollow tube. It has two ear pieces and a listening part at the other end. It makes sounds seem louder.

Books to Read

The Amazing Pull-Up Pop-Up Body in a Book by Caroline Bingham and Penny Smith (Dorling Kindersley, 1997)

A Tudor Medicine Chest by Brian Moses (Wayland, 1997)

A Victorian Hospital by Katrina Siliprandi (Wayland, 1994)

Going to the Doctor by Ann Civardi and Stephen Cartwright (Usborne, 1992)

How Our Bodies Work series by Carol Ballard (Wayland, 1997)

What's Wrong With Me? by Jenny Bryan (Wayland, 1994)

Editor: Sarah Doughty
Cover designer: Jan Sterling
Designer and typesetter: Malcolm Walker

Dedicated to a baby called Mark

First published in 1998 by
Wayland Publishers Ltd
61 Western Road, Hove
East Sussex, BN3 1JD

© Copyright 1998 Wayland Publishers Ltd

British Library Cataloguing in Publication Data

Harbour, Janet
 People who help us in hospital
 1. Hospitals – Staff – Juvenile literature
 I. Title II. In Hospital
 610.6'9

ISBN 0 7502 2251 4

Printed and bound by EuroGrafica, Vicenza, Italy

Find Wayland on the Internet at http://www.wayland.co.uk

Index

Picture acknowledgements
Impact 4, 5 (Peter Arkell), 6 (Charles Milligan), 7 (Peter Arkell), 9 (Tom Webster), 10 (Peter Arkell), 11 (Piers Cavendish), 12 (Peter Arkell), 13 (Piers Cavendish), 16 (Bruce Stephens), 17 (Julian Calder), 18 (Caroline Penn), 19 (John Cole), 20 (Mike McQueen), 25 bottom (John Cole), 26 (Mike McQueen), 27 bottom (Mike McQueen); Science Photo Library 15 (John Greim); Wayland Picture Library 3, 8, 14 (Andrew Perris), 21 (Andrew Perris), 22 (Andrew Perris), 23 (Andrew Perris), 24 (Andrew Perris), 25 top (Andrew Perris), 27 top (Eye Ubiquitous). Cover pictures: Main picture Impact (Charles Milligan), all other pictures are from the Wayland Picture Library (Andrew Perris, APM).